OLD AMERICA

Plantations

Lynn Stone

Rourke Publications, Inc.
Vero Beach, FL 32964

Edited by Sandra A. Robinson

PHOTO CREDITS
© Gene Ahrens: cover, title page, 4, 6, 14, 20, 21, 22, 25, 29;
© Lynn M. Stone: 13, 27; © James P. Rowan: 16, 28, 30;
 courtesy U.S. Army Military History Institute: 7, 8, 11, 18.

Library of Congress Cataloging-in-Publication Data

Stone, Lynn M.
  Plantations / by Lynn Stone.
  p. cm. — (Old America)
  Summary: Discusses the lifestyle of the large plantations in America's Old South and gives some notable examples, including Mount Vernon, Monticello, and Mississippi's Magnolia Hall.
  ISBN 0-86625-446-3
  1. Plantations – Southern States – Juvenile literature.
2. Plantation life – Southern States – History – Juvenile literature.
[1. Plantation life – Southern States. 2. Plantations – Southern States. 3. Southern States – Social life and customs – 1775-1865.] I. Title. II. Series: Stone, Lynn M. Old America.
F210.S75 1993
975—dc20   93-771
                                                   CIP
                                                   AC

Printed in the USA

TABLE OF CONTENTS

I PLANTATIONS

*Mt. Vernon was the plantation home of George Washington,
America's first president and a wealthy Virginia planter.*

They lived in grand style, like kings and queens. They attended grand balls and cultivated lush gardens. They rode fine horses and built incredibly beautiful riverfront homes. They were the **planters**, the owners of great, sprawling **plantations** in America's Old South.

A plantation was a large farm. It was also a center of **commerce**, or trade. The plantation marketed its own farm crops and sometimes sold crops bought from other farms.

The plantation lifestyle was unique to the Old South, which included the states of Maryland, Virginia, Georgia, South Carolina, North Carolina, Tennessee, Florida, Alabama, Mississippi, Louisiana and eastern Texas. Plantations began to appear in the 1600s, shortly after the South was settled by English colonists. Plantations continued to spread throughout the South until 1861. That was the beginning of the American Civil War, also known as the War Between the States. When the war ended in 1865, the plantation lifestyle ended, too.

The largest plantations were showplaces of wealth and power. Their glory years were before the war, an era in Southern history known as the **antebellum** period. Many of the **mansions**, the big homes of the planters, were modeled after Greek temples with tall, white columns. The lane leading to the mansion was sometimes a leafy tunnel formed by an archway of oaks. The mansion at lane's end and the trailing beards of Spanish

A lane under spreading oaks leads to antebellum Boone Hall Plantation in South Carolina.

moss on trees created an unforgettable image of quiet beauty.

Many people believe that the antebellum South was a land of one great plantation after another. The truth is, though, the typical Southerner in the prewar South didn't own a plantation. He or she was not likely to even visit one. Plantation owners, the "true" planters, made up a very small and special class of people. To be considered a planter, a man had to own 20 slaves. Most of the planters did not have huge plantations. As war neared in 1860, only about 2,300 Southerners — one man in 500 — owned 100 or more slaves and a large plantation. The men in this group were the truly wealthy planters. Their grand life of ease and elegance was certainly not shared by the slaves who worked their plantations — or the thousands of poor white Southern farmers.

Although plantations had certain things in common, each was unique. Few plantation owners ever equalled the holdings of Robert "King" Carter of Virginia. He owned 1,000 slaves and 330,000 acres of land — more land than Grand Teton National Park! Some of the richest planters grew sugar cane. In Louisiana, it used to be said that a man had to be a *rich* cotton planter before he could begin to be a *poor* sugar planter. The wealthiest Louisiana sugar planters lived like kings.

Slave quarters stand along the soft, sandy road leading to the plantation of Confederate general T.F. Drayton on Hilton Head, South Carolina.

Former slaves plant sweet potatoes at James Hopkinson's plantation on Edisto Island, South Carolina. This photograph was taken in 1862, shortly after they had been freed by the Union Army.

Many people wanted to be planters. Their way of life was widely admired. Planters had wealth, property and power. Unfortunately, much of their wealth was built upon someone else's **poverty.** Plantations ran largely because of the unpaid labor of slaves. Slaves were "owned" by the planters. They were bought and sold like wagons and horses.

II THE RISE OF PLANTATIONS AND SLAVERY

*The stately "big house" of James Hopkinson and the plantation
that surrounded it were maintained by slaves.*

It did not take English colonists long to turn Southern soil into productive farmland. For more than 200 days each year, there was no threat of frost. Profitable crops such as rice, sugar cane, cotton and tobacco thrived. The larger the farm, the more money a man could make.

The plantations began during America's Colonial period (1607-1783), before the British colonies in America became states. Many of the plantations were started by wealthy Englishmen who were given land by the British government. The export of plantation crops to England became a profitable business.

Planters who were wealthy enough to own large plantations needed a large labor force to make the plantations successful. The number of colonists was limited. The solution to the labor problem was the use of African slaves, who were first brought to Virginia as early as 1619. As the 17th century wore on, slave labor became increasingly important. The number of plantations grew. Slaves, or "bondsmen" as they were sometimes called, provided cheap labor.

By 1790, slaves made up about one-third of the entire Southern population. The plantation system spread westward into Louisiana, Mississippi, Tennessee and east Texas. Like an incurable disease, slavery traveled with it.

The early Virginia planters from Britain brought with them a tradition of class distinction. The planters were generally part of the British **aristocracy**, the

Slave cabins, like these in South Carolina, were often located some distance from the planter's big house.

upper, ruling class. In Britain, aristocracy was based on the wealth and power that land ownership provided. Those who were not born into Britain's aristocracy were not likely to ever join it. It would not be much different in the Old South.

The fact that a plantation's successful operation depended upon slaves was not a problem for most of the planters. In their eyes, some people were born to rule, others to work. In their eyes, slaves were probably viewed as a lower form of life. As time passed, some plantation owners — Thomas Jefferson, for one — felt uncomfortable with slavery. Others continued to

Thomas Jefferson, the nation's third president, held slaves at Monticello, his Virginia plantation.

The quiet, slow-paced life in the plantation big houses was doomed when Southern states left the Union.

believe in the grim fairy tale that slaves were inferior people and should be kept in bondage. Now and then, slaves were given their freedom. Still, slavery was an abuse of human rights, regardless of how "caring" a master may have been. Because they could be bought and sold, slaves faced uncertain futures. Families were sometimes separated at slave sales.

An American aristocracy developed in the Old South, with a wealthy ruling class of planters. Their big houses were showplaces of power and wealth as they stood tall above the land and the slave quarters. Ships sailed to the private docks of riverside plantations. Slaves unloaded furniture, fine china, spices, silverware and wine, then reloaded the ships with tobacco, lumber, cotton and other plantation products.

In 1860, about 2 million of the South's more than 3 million slaves lived on plantations. The plantation system was at its peak. Meanwhile, the Northern states were rapidly becoming more **industrial**. Factories boomed. The lives of people in the North and South were very different. Many Northerners loudly objected to the Southern practice of slavery. Slavery had become an open, ugly wound, but the plantation landlords were dependent upon the ways of the Old South. They knew that they could not afford to run huge plantations if they had to pay free men to work. They wanted no part of a different world.

By 1862, John Seabrook's plantation on Edisto Island — and the private wharf on which the Army photographer stood — had been taken over by Union soldiers, some of whom are in the rowboat.

A big plantation was **self-sufficient.** It furnished everything it needed — water, bricks, firewood, milk, meat, vegetables, cloth, leather goods, furniture and other necessities. Slaves kept up the plantation's many buildings and performed a variety of tasks, from sawing wood to hammering and fitting horseshoes.

The plantation's main job was to produce a "cash" crop — a farm product that could be sold to earn money for the planter. In much of the inland South, cotton was the chief crop. Along the rivers and inlets of Chesapeake Bay, tobacco plantations prospered. South Carolina and Georgia planters in the marshy lowlands specialized in rice. Sugar was the cash king in much of Louisiana.

Field slaves planted, weeded and eventually harvested the cash crop. They worked under the direction of **overseers** hired by the planter. Plantations also raised food for the people and animals on the plantation. **Domestic**, or house, slaves cooked and served meals. They also maintained the mansions, some of which had 50 or more rooms.

The planter himself often traveled on business. The day-to-day operation of the plantation was left to the overseers. The planter's wife was often called upon to entertain guests, and many a wife became a knowledge-able businesswoman in her husband's absence. The planter's children attended school on a plantation, either their own or at a plantation nearby.

Rosedown Plantation and many other Louisiana estates survived the fury and destruction of the Civil War.

During the Civil War, the quiet, comfortable life of the plantation changed dramatically. Some of the planters' wives and children faced nearly as much hardship as their slaves did. With husbands at war, women helped to scavenge food and nurse wounded soldiers. Both the Northern and Southern armies sometimes turned plantation houses into hospitals.

IV THE FALL OF PLANTATIONS

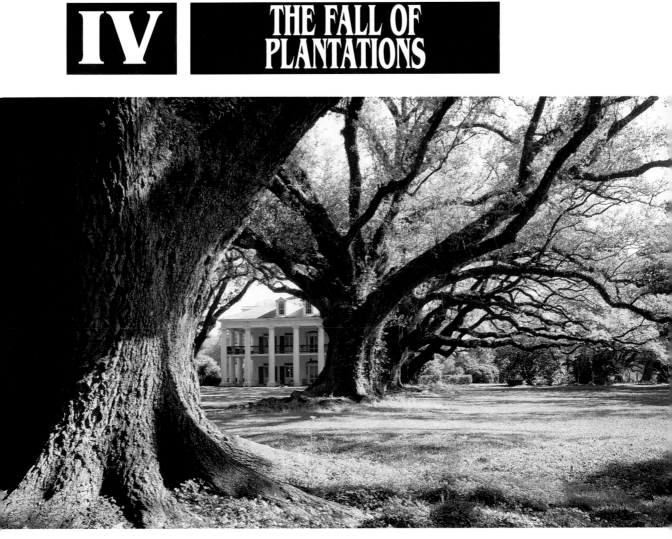

Oak Alley Plantation in Vacherie, Louisiana, was another of the sugar plantations spared from warfare.

Unlike many of its less fortunate neighbors, Boone Hall survived the vicious warfare in South Carolina.

The North and South had argued for years, mostly about the future of slavery. Eventually, the South began to feel its way of life was being threatened by the industrial North. It was expected that new states admitted to the Union would oppose slavery. The South was becoming a smaller and smaller minority in the United States Congress.

By early 1861, 11 angry Southern states had **seceded** — removed themselves from the Union. The slavery issue aside, President Abraham Lincoln warned the Southern states that they did not have the right to leave the United States. The new Confederate States of America, made up of the breakaway states, ignored Mr.

Lincoln's warning. The North and South launched into a terrible civil war in April, 1861. It lasted four years, and more than 600,000 American soldiers — Northern and Southern, black and white — died.

The armies at war destroyed many plantation buildings. Along the Ashley River in South Carolina, once a sort of "plantation row," just one mansion survived the war. The great palaces of the sugar kings in Louisiana were generally spared because most of the fighting took place in the southeast. Even so, the days of the sugar plantations were over. The sugar market and cheap slave labor vanished.

Southern plantations that survived the war failed because new competition from foreign countries caused market prices to sag. With prices down and slavery finished, almost no one could afford to keep a huge plantation and home. Plantations were divided and sold. Big houses were often deserted. Paint faded and peeled. Mold gathered, and dirt drifted through broken windows. Vines strangled the once proud columns. In time, many of the big houses burned or crumbled away.

A few places were spared. Their owners continued to produce crops, although not at prewar levels. Some of the surviving mansions became offices, hospitals, restaurants, hotels or homes for new owners.

The Civil War changed the United States. The plantation homes that remained were the leftovers of a different time. By war's end, the plantation system had unraveled like a ball of cotton yarn.

V PLANTATIONS: A TOUR

Most plantation houses today stand on only a few of the acres that the estate once covered.

Most of the **restored**, or repaired, antebellum plantations occupy far fewer acres than they once did. If you visit plantations, do not expect to see the great homes rise from a sea of cotton or tobacco. After all, few of the former plantations are still working farms. Today, visiting a plantation usually means visiting the restored plantation home and its showy gardens.

Saved by individuals and various organizations, some of the old plantation homes again show their former beauty and charm. Visiting one of them is a journey into the Old South. Dozens of homes are open to the public. Here is just a sampling of Southern plantation homes:

In Florida, visitors can inspect a mansion at the Gamble Plantation Site in Ellenton, or a modest planter's house at the Kingsley Plantation Site on Fort George Island. In Georgia, the Antebellum Plantation at Stone Mountain Park in Atlanta is a re-created plantation. Florewood River Plantation State Park in Greenwood, Mississippi, is also a **re-creation**.

Mississippi has many original plantations, too, including Magnolia Hall and Longwood in Natchez. According to folklore, Magnolia Hall was struck by a shell fired from a Northern gunboat during the Civil War. The shell exploded in a pot, leaving the plantation diners with soup burns.

A trail of plantations leads from Baton Rouge to New Orleans, Louisiana. Nottoway, with 64 rooms, is the

Florida's Gamble Plantation in Ellenton shows off Greek columns.

Northern construction workers who were building the Longwood Plantation house left their jobs and returned home when war broke out between the states.

South's largest remaining plantation home. Oak Alley's mansion is approached through a lane shaded by oaks planted in the early 1700s. Chalmette Plantation is part of the Jean Lafitte National Historic Park. American General Andrew Jackson defeated British troops there in the Battle of New Orleans in January, 1815.

In Charleston, South Carolina, Boone Hall Plantation and nearby Magnolia Garden Plantation have magnificent gardens. In North Carolina, the Orton Plantation graces coastal Wilmington. Latta Plantation Park in Huntersville overlooks the Catawba River.

Spring flowers blossom in the gardens of Mount Vernon.

A cannon stands on the old Chalmette Plantation grounds where an American army defeated the British in the Battle of New Orleans.

Two of the most famous plantation sites in America, Mount Vernon and Monticello, are in Virginia. Mount Vernon was the home of America's first president, George Washington. Thomas Jefferson, the third president, lived at Monticello. Among other major plantations in Virginia are Oatlands, Shirley, Berkeley, Carter's Grove and Gunston Hall.

GLOSSARY

antebellum (ant eh BELL um) - existing before the American Civil War

aristocracy (air iss TOHK ruh see) - the upper, ruling class in a society

commerce (KAH murss) - the trade of goods and services

domestic (duhm ESS tihk) - relating to the home

industrial (in DUS tree uhl) - having to do with the manufacture of products

mansion (MAN shun) - a large and expensive home

overseer (O ver see er) - one who is responsible for the smooth operation of a business; one who directs others and their activities

plantation (plan TAY shun) - in the Old South, a large farm that produced crops and acted as a center of commerce

planter (PLAN ter) - in the Old South, one who owned at least 20 slaves and operated a plantation

poverty (PAH ver tee) - the state of having very little money and owning few possessions

re-creation (ree kree A shun) - something that has been created to be identical to an original thing, such as a re-created building

restored (re STORD) - renewed, returned to the original condition

secede (seh SEED) - to withdraw from an organization

self-sufficient (SELF suh FISH ent) - able to provide for one's own needs

INDEX